POIRET

© 2006 Assouline Publishing
601 West 26th Street, 18th floor
New York, NY 10001, USA
Tel.: 212 989-6810   Fax: 212 647-0005
www.assouline.com

First published in Great Britain, in 1997,
by Thames and Hudson Ltd, London
© 1997 Assouline Publishing

Translated from the French by Caroline Beamish

ISBN: 978 2 7594 0100 0

Color separation: Gravor (Switzerland)
Printed by Grafiche Milani (Italy)

FRANÇOIS BAUDOT

ASSOULINE

t he twentieth century was only ten years old when Paul Poiret's career was at its height. A cosmopolitan group of artists, including Guillaume Apollinaire, Igor Stravinsky, Pablo Picasso, Alberto Santos-Dumont, Jean Cocteau, Sergei Diaghilev, and Misia Sert had assembled in Paris to reinvent the century. Between the completion of Picasso's *Demoiselles d'Avignon* (1907) and the first performance of Stravinsky's *The Rite of Spring* (1913), the group laid the foundations of the avant-garde. In the meantime, Poiret had undressed and dressed his generation, confirming his position as a highly revolutionary and innovative couturier, a reputation that still holds today.

Poiret was born rotund and cheerful—a Parisian to his fingertips—on April 8, 1879, in Les Halles. His parents were cloth merchants with a business "à l'Enseigne de l'Espérance" (at the sign of Good Hope), an attribute, incidentally, which their son never lost. Even when he was old and poor, the great couturier would recount the *Fables of la Fontaine* to fellow diners in the bistros where he was a regular customer; one of his favorite tales was "The Grasshopper and the Ant," which he recited with the hindsight of experience. Poiret packed a wide range of activities into his life, and his remarkable influence stretched far beyond the world of fashion. Even today, his achievements seem extraordinary.

Poiret was a gifted child, lovingly adored by his mother and his three sisters. He soon showed signs of a vivid imagination, which was accompanied by a kind of waywardness and curiosity. Parisian life distracted

5

him from his studies at an early age without, however, preventing him from gaining his baccalaureate. In order (so he said) to break the boy's pride, his father sent him off with his certificate in his pocket to a job as a delivery boy for a firm of umbrella makers. By now, Poiret was a passionate draftsman and eager for experience of all kinds, his head teeming with ideas. It is easy to see how he might have chafed at the bit as, dressed in overalls, he carried a great box of umbrellas on his back. In fact, throughout his life, he continually grumbled, ironically, of course, about the failure of his fellow men to appreciate his worth. At some point, his sisters gave him a small wooden figure, about two inches high, and to their amazement, he took out all his frustration on this doll. In his room, during the evenings, he fashioned stunning outfits out of scraps of silk he picked up in the umbrella factory. According to Poiret, the *Parisienne* was born during these lamp lit evenings spent at home.

b uilt for the Exposition Universelle in 1889 and situated on the banks of the Seine River, the Eiffel Tower was a visible symbol of progress. Yet, one hundred years after the storming of the Bastille, the appearance of women of fashion had not changed at all. Though the abolition of the whalebone corset was urgently recommended by doctors (on medical grounds) and by suffragettes (on principle), the waistline still remained firmly in place, as it had since the Renaissance.

During this time, the female body was divided into two independent halves, like an hourglass, and permitted little freedom of movement. Although fashions in the design, colors, and trimmings of costume had developed along lines imposed by the most dazzling court in Europe, the basic structure of clothes had remained the same for six hundred years, apart from a brief respite during the Revolution, when there was a return to fluid shapes, draped fabrics, and light, clinging gowns.

In 1900, when Poiret first began to consider choosing fashion as his way of giving expression to the desire for change, young women still resembled fragile birds, or slender vines, with long necks topped by a bouffant hairstyle. The bust was well padded and prominent, the waist neatly nipped in, and the figure draped in laces and silks of pale shades. With their moral straitjackets and whalebone corsets, these women resembled creatures painted by the likes of Paul Helleu and Giovanni Boldini.

J acques Doucet was the great master of late nineteenth-century fashion. A man of enormous distinction, he directed his own fashion house in the rue de la Paix, though, in fact, the fashion designing was mainly left to his staff. Paul Poiret showed his sketches to Doucet and the latter, one of the most notable collectors of contemporary art of his day, and also a well-informed bibliophile (he set up library of art history that bears his name, the first of its kind), had the good sense to engage him as his assistant. Poiret stayed on for four years. Under Doucet's tutelage, this draper's son was transformed into a designer of taste, and became well grounded in the intricacies of the profession. Poiret the couturier was already beginning to show through, and he was impatient for progress. Having completed his national service, he went to work for Worth, the most prestigious fashion house of the period. He perfected his knowledge of high fashion during his time spent here.

In 1903, Madame Poiret lent her son fifty thousand francs and he set himself up independently to design the kind of dresses he was itching to make on his own. Réjane, the great actress, whom he had dressed at

Doucet, followed him. The presence of his celebrated team of two white mules—a gift from the King of Portugal—in front of his boutique on rue Auber was a great help in launching the new business. To start with, Poiret simplified clothes. Upon marrying Denise Boulet, an unspoilt young woman from the provinces, he began experimenting with bold designs, which were created just for her. Denise bore him five children, of whom three survived. Her admiration for her impetuous husband was unstinting and she soon became one of the leading ladies of the new fashion. In 1906, the Directoire line, promoted by Poiret, burst onto the scene of an unsuspecting fashion world. The waist rose to meet the bosom, and skirts fell straight from the waist to the ankles. The couturier encouraged his clients to abandon the whalebone corset in favor of a broad, stiffened belt. Perhaps the reintroduction of the hobble skirt was not a great contribution to liberty. Nevertheless, in spite of everything, the relaxation of dress was complete within a few years and the softened lines were unanimously adopted.

●

In 1909, Orientalism was the fashion. The first season of the Ballets Russes in Paris ignited Poiret's imagination. Wide-brimmed hats and frock coats gave way to turbans and caftans, and colors became brighter and more eye-catching. Poiret, the new caliph, erected his tent in the rue du Faubourg Saint-Honoré, ignoring solemn warnings that no one was likely to go shopping in that residential quarter. The clothes in his new collection, which were the talk of the town, were borrowed from all over the world: geisha kimonos, trousers as worn by Egyptian dancing girls, Ukranian peasant costumes, silks and perfumes from Arabia, and Greek costumes as revived by Isadora Duncan. Most of the trends that later exerted a permanent influence on today's great designers can be traced back to Poiret's fabulous bazaar.

Poiret's years, though relatively short, were prolific, crucial, and uncompromising, allowing this born businessman to develop his extraordinary talent in many different artistic directions. Besides raising the status of a profession into an independent art form, this great innovator continually explored and developed new avenues. The field of his activities was what we now call the "art of living," and none of the applied arts was excluded from it.

t en years before Chanel, Poiret realized the advantages of a couturier manufacturing and marketing his own fragrances. The French perfume industry, based on the distillation of floral essences in the area around Grasse, was still monopolized by perfume manufacturers. Poiret launched Les Parfums de Rosine, named after his elder daughter, with individual perfumes like "Bosquet d'Apollon," "Le fruit défendu," "Aladin," "Chez Poiret," "Le mouchoir de Rosine," and so forth. Each bottle was linked to a particular gown and designed to be a work of art. The perfume itself, on the other hand, now made generous use of science, thanks to developments that made it possible to recreate all of nature's basic scents in the laboratory. With the assistance of a chemist, Doctor Midy, a friend from his schooldays, Poiret put on his overalls once again, this time with great enthusiasm.

Poiret's perfume-making factory, based in Courbevoie, soon entered into partnership with the glassworks factory where the bottles were made. A cardboard factory, which specialized in highly original packaging, completed the trinity. Poiret hired highly skilled and talented artists, writers, typographers, and model-makers to design the publicity and promotional materials for the different Rosine perfumes. For its time, this was a revolutionary method of advertising. As the accessory and cosmetic businesses took off, Poiret signed his first licensing agreements.

In 1909, Poiret moved into a handsome eighteenth-century residence on the Avenue d'Antin, now Avenue Franklin-Roosevelt. Following in the footsteps of his mentor, Jacques Doucet, the now-famous Poiret became a collector and supporter of modern art; his salons were extravagently restored by the architect Louis Süe.

Although as a painter, Poiret could not have been more traditional, he collected Francis Picabia, Andre Dunoyer de Segonzac, Kees van Dongen, and all the other greatest living artists. Many of these artists were his friends and collaborated with him on various projects: from assisting in the promotion of his products to interior design to creating extravagant parties and entertainment spectacles. Between 1908 and 1911, with two of the most remarkable illustrators of the twentieth century, Paul Iribe and Paul Lepape, Poiret established a collaboration that exemplified other working relationships between himself and artists. He was the catalyst of many fashion ventures of the day. He employed Erté, whom he had encountered in Russia, as a fashion illustrator, as well as Mariano Fortuny, before the latter retired to Venice to pursue his research into fabric and light. But his most productive alliance was with the young Raoul Dufy, who was just beginning his career. Poiret commissioned designs from Dufy that were to change the course of fabric design and fabric printing for the worlds of both fashion and furnishing.

Inspired by the spirit of the Vienna Secession to participate in all existing creative fields, Poiret was soon involved in every branch of the decorative arts: interior design, printing, embroidery, haberdashery, furniture, lighting, as well as clothes and accessories. In 1914, he set up an art school for talented but impoverished girls, which he called "Martine" after his second daughter. Students were taught to express themselves with a creative freedom that still seems amazing. A year later a shop, also called "Martine," was established in the rue du Faubourg Saint-Honoré; it sold exclusive carpets, textiles, lamps and light fittings, vases, wallpaper, furniture, and assorted ornaments. The "Martines," as they were nicknamed, were a great success. Several department stores opened Martine counters—in London, Berlin, and Philadelphia, among others. The illustrated press featured several of the group's interiors, thus guaranteeing their influence on 1920s design.

t he parties given by Poiret and his wife in one or another of their houses were never forgotten by those fortunate enough to be invited. The "Thousand and Second Night" party, on June 24, 1911, was an Oriental extravaganza attended by all of Paris. The decor was by Raoul Dufy and Poiret himself designed the costumes. Instead of spending enormous sums on advertising, the dress designer preferred to gather together a few hundred distinguished guests and provide them with an experience they would never forget. Today, we call this kind of strategizing public relations.

Poiret's parties have never been rivaled in the annals of Parisian life. Less is known about the expensive experiment called "The Oasis," in which an open-air room was constructed in the peaceful, leafy garden of the Poiret residence, a stone's throw from the Champs-Élysées. In the summer, Poiret organized entertainment for his friends and relations and their guests in The Oasis. To guard against rain, he asked Voisin, the designer and builder of motorcars, to create a huge inflatable structure made out of the rubber then used for aircrafts. The pneumatic dome rose above the height of the trees and protected the spectators as they relaxed in their multi-colored armchairs.

The turn-of-the-century optimism that Poiret embraced and in many respects embodied, was soon dispersed in the battle trenches of Verdun. Poiret was called up and served his country as a tailor for nearly five years. After some memorable adventures, he ended the Great War with the rank of captain. Violence did not suit this good-natured man at all. When he returned to Paris after the Armistice, his fashion house had closed down, his property was mortgaged, and his health had been affected by the war. France was impoverished and Poiret had to start all over again. But some things had changed for the better, too: salaries and textile prices had risen, demands were different, and a new, active woman had taken over from the *houris* of the pre-war period.

Poiret the great innovator may have created the first dresses that could be put on without assistance; he may have narrowed the silhouette and made it lighter; he may have forged the way forward for all his successors, but he felt nothing but aversion for the urchin look. He loathed the undernourished telegraph boy dressed in black jersey, now proposed to women by the disquieting and severe Madame Chanel. Although not yet forty years old, Poiret seemed to belong to another world. He had rejected the Belle Époque and now the twenties, "The Crazy Years," were giving him a hard time. Fashion lavishes praise on anyone who is ten years ahead, but never forgives anyone who is ten minutes late.

Although success now began to elude him, Poiret made no effort to reduce his lifestyle or to trim the out-of-date extravagance of his collections. But Yvonne Deslandres, founder of the Musée de la Mode at the Union Centrale des Arts Décoratifs and a great specialist on Poiret, believes that the great couturier did his best and most original work after the 1914-1918 war. His gowns were less full of references and less aggressive than before, retaining only the essence of his wide-ranging research into antiquity, the Orient, Symbolism, and so on. He combined refinement with abstraction and sophistication with extreme modernity. It is obvious that the Poiret models so carefully preserved in the Musée de la Mode et du Textile have left their mark on the work of contemporary designers, such as Yves Saint Laurent, Issey Miyake, Kenzo, Romeo Gigli, Yohji Yamamoto; and, most explicitly of all, on John Galliano.

before the First World War, Poiret replaced black (and white) stockings with flesh-colored ones and developed the suspender belt to hold them up. He also promoted the girdle, which by this time had replaced the corset. Thanks to these three innovations, the curve of the leg was revealed for the first time— by no means an unimportant development. In addition, it was he who put women's breasts into the "soft harness" of the bust bodice, or brassiere. After this, having made the slender silhouette fashionable, he launched the sheath dress, the sack dress, and the culotte skirt, and these simplified shapes inevitably brought with them an economy of design, at any rate in comparison with the extravagance of the Second Empire or the Belle Époque.

Poiret's worldview was a comprehensive one. As a megalomaniac (albeit a very human one) he wished all the young women he adored to be dressed like fine ladies. He was intrigued by America and made several successful visits there, establishing contacts with the big stores and their buyers. He evolved, reaching a much larger market by creating so-called export models—a means of licensed reproduction, which took other fashion houses thirty years to adopt. Only firms agreeing to sell his models could use the Poiret label, and royalties would be payable on each model reproduced. It seems obvious today, but it was revolutionary at the time. Poiret was aware of the high stakes competition represented by the United States from the outset; his response to the challenge was to organize big promotional tours, taking his most seductive models with him to tempt the Americans. The Armistice seems to have increased America's influence over Europe and accelerated Europe's hitherto latent tendency toward democratization. In the face of this wave of change, Poiret's response was very French: as an admirer of progress, he wished everything to change, but as a conservative he wished everything to stay the same. With remarkable ingenuity, he laid down the basis for reform, but his inability to make any practical use of it made him its victim.

I n 1924, in collaboration with the publisher Albin Michel, Poiret began to produce a weekly magazine. This contained original Poiret patterns with descriptions, and bore the catchphrase "Elegance is no longer a question of money"—a motto that might well have been used unaltered by Hélène Lazareff when she created the magazine *Elle* in 1947. Any reader taking out a subscription to Poiret's magazine received a pair of his flesh-colored stockings. (The color was politely called "champagne.") Winners of a magazine-sponsored competition were rewarded with a designer dress by Poiret. In 1933, the proprietor of Au Printemps, the department store, made a suggestion to Poiret, who by that time had lost his own fashion house, that he guaranteed would be a success.

For a hefty monthly fee, Monsieur Poiret was persuaded to present four collections a year, one per season, inside the shop, and to charge "factory" prices for the clothes. Au Printemps would take care of the publicity and the catwalk . . . and eventually the applause, music, and champagne that came with fame. This short-lived experiment (Poiret soon began to realize he was being exploited) marked the beginning of designer prêt-à-porter shows as we know them today. It was not until the 1950s, however, that fashion shows such as these became the norm.

the year 1925—a key year in contemporary history and in Parisian life—should have seen Paul Poiret at his zenith, but by one of those paradoxes that seemed to dog the great couturier's footsteps, the year of the "années folles" coincided with his swansong. Abandoned by his followers, harassed by his creditors, misused by fame and incapable of reform, Poiret had to sell off his assets. He sold the residence in the Avenue d'Antin and moved round the corner to the Rond-Point des Champs-Élysées, where the Carven boutique is today. Meanwhile he sold the name Poiret to his associates, who showed little respect for the designer's past feats of imagination.

Nevertheless, "Poiret Rond-Point" was the first fashion house to use indirect lighting and to have an illuminated shop front; it sold accessories and sport clothes under the label "Bagatelles", merchandise late to be sold in what came to be called the "boutique" department of large stores. At the first meeting of the board of directors, Poiret announced proudly that his house would be participating in the great exhibition of decorative arts and modern industry—the exhibition to which the Art Deco style owes its name. Over the previous twenty years, no one had given so much impetus to the luxury goods trade; Poiret saw the great exhibition as a tacit endorsement of his visionary qualities and an exemplification of his lifelong claim that craft was also art. It also demonstrated the opposite—that luxury goods could be mass-produced.

Seventy-two dress designers took part in the exhibition. Not to be outdone, Poiret hired three barges—*Amours*, *Délices* and *Orgues*—to ply up and down the Seine; they were the highlight of the event. *Délices*, decorated by Martine, was devoted (as the name suggests) to food and gastronomy. *Orgues* was completely decorated in white. The couture collection was modeled in relays, and the walls were decorated with fourteeen original frescoes by Raoul Dufy, which showed views of Paris in a jumble of perspectives. *Amours* featured the latest fragrances by "Rosine." Success was immediate and enormous, but so was the financial fall-out. Poiret's partners had refused to share the expenses of the extravaganza and Poiret himself was forced to finance the whole operation. It was a financial burden from which he never fully recovered. Consumed by debt, Poiret made a grand, unforgettable stage debut in 1925, thanks to his dear friend Colette. She had just adapted her novel *The Vagabond* for the theater and gave Poiret the role of the second male lead, acting next to Marguerite Moréno and Pierre-Auguste Renoir. The presence of the dress designer immediately turned the opening night into a great event. The run lasted for a fortnight and Poiret donated most of his fee to a home for artists' orphaned children.

Paul Poiret's professional life came to an end in the early 1930s. Stouter, and more of a fantasist than ever, he lived for a time in a vast Art Deco apartment overlooking the Salle Pleyel. Here he hung all the works of art that he had not yet sold. The larder was bare. To keep himself busy, he compiled a recipe book, entitled *107 Recettes ou curiosités culinaires* (which included a recipe for "a salad for the new poor"), complete with one hundred and seven illustrations by Marie Alix. Always with pen in hand, he wrote for various magazines, advancing his point of view on various matters, like "Phynance" or "the art of the party." Finally, he presented Bernard Grasset, his friend and publisher, with the manuscript of an admirable book of memoirs, *En habillant l'époque*, which is still in print.

L ife continued until the Second World War. Poiret sold everything, including the drawings of the Cubist house designed for him by Robert Mallet-Stevens on a bend in the Seine River. In 1944, during the bitter period of the German occupation of Paris, he revealed yet another facet of his paintings, and on March 11, the Galerie Charpentier held an exhibition of his new collection. Though pale and thin (he had lost seventy-seven pounds), Poiret was his magnificent self, buzzing with ideas, plans, and enthusiasm. In the introduction to the catalogue, Jean Cocteau heaps praise on the man who liberated women. Cheered though he was, Poiret was not to witness the liberation of France. Some days before his sixty-fifth birthday he died—an event that was met with general indifference. He was convinced to his dying day that he was just going through a bad patch, and that nobody understood him. Let us hope that this book, though written posthumously, will restore his legacy.

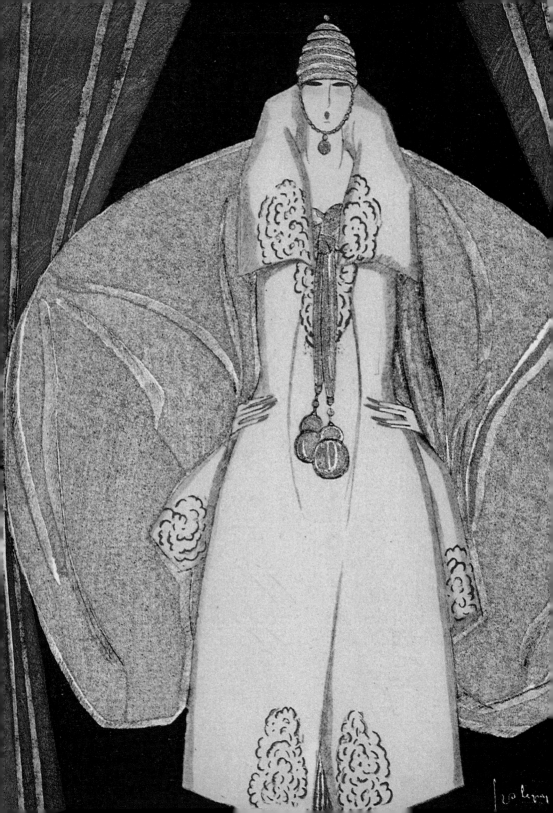

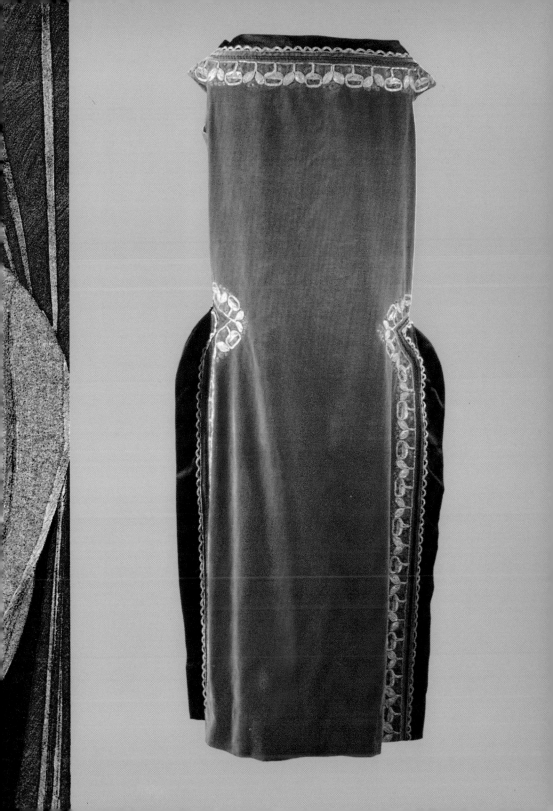

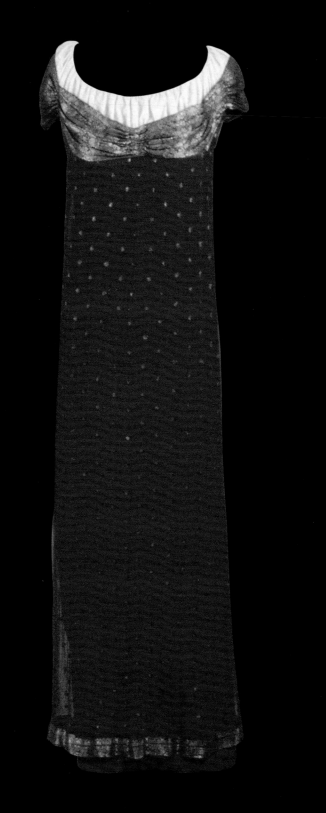

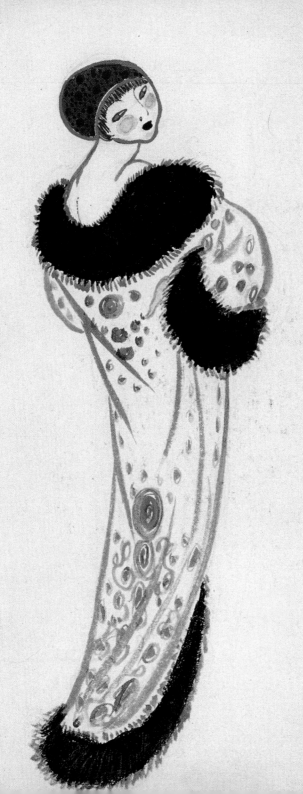

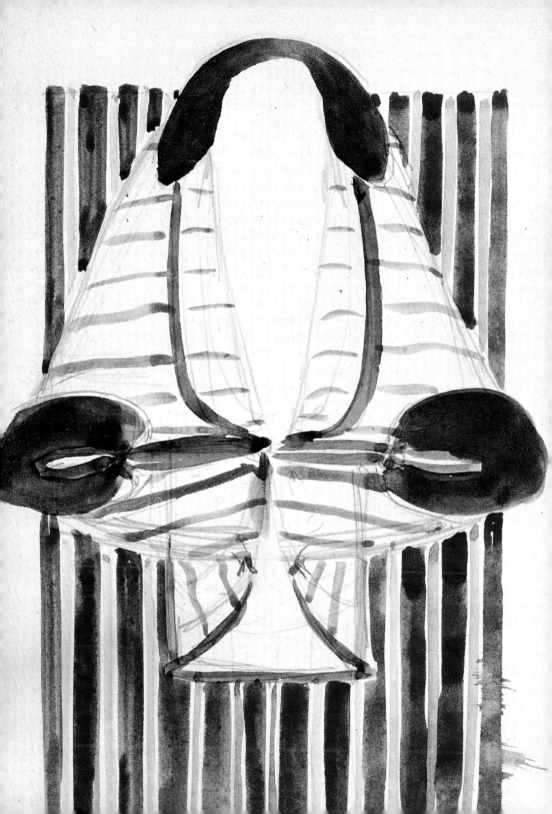

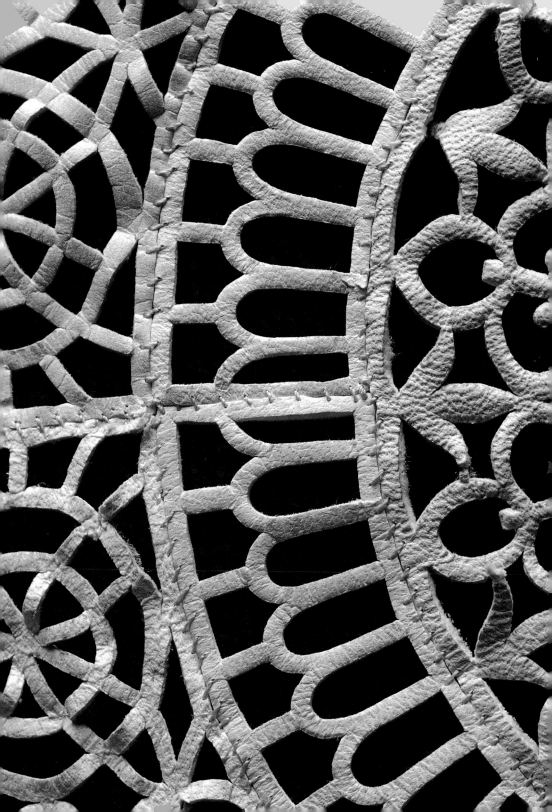

© 1913
Geisler
Bauma

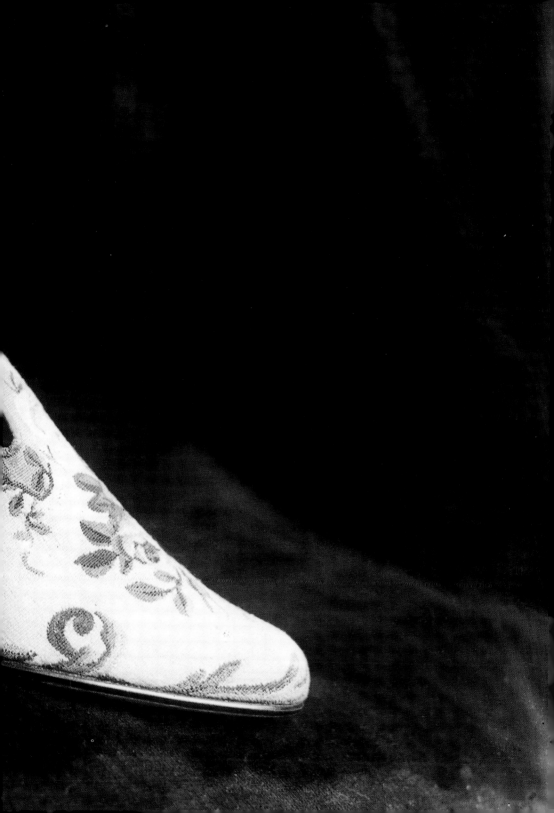

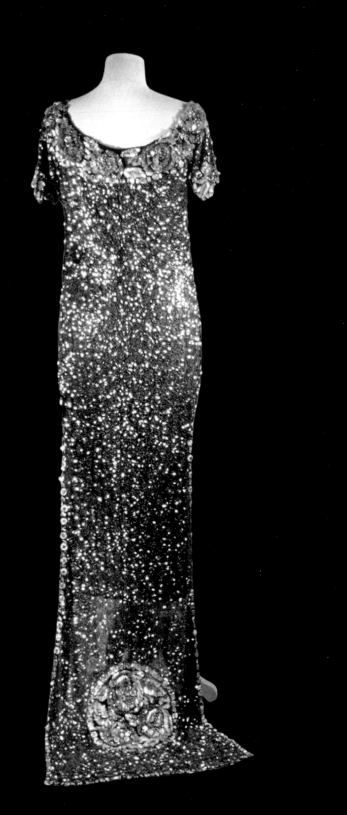

Chronology

1879   Born in Paris, in Les Halles, where his parents were cloth merchants in the Ruelle des Deux Eures (no longer extant).

1897   Poiret discovers the magic of the Orient – at a carpet exhibition at the Bon Marché. He is apprenticed to a firm of umbrella makers at the time.

1889   He is hired by the celebrated couturier Jacques Doucet, to whom he had shown his portfolio of fashion sketches. Réjane and many other fashionable actresses of the day were Doucet's clients; here Poiret learns the advantages and disadvantages of working in the fashion business.

1901   After national service, Paul Poiret moves to the largest fashion house of the day, Worth, at the age of twenty-two. Here he perfects his knowledge of the profession.

1903   With his mother's savings and plenty of optimism, the young couturier opens his own fashion house at 5 Rue Auber. Réjane is his first customer.

1905   Poiret marries Denise Boulet, a pretty girl from the provinces, and a childhood friend. She would become Poiret's model and one of the most elegant women in Paris.

1906   Opening of the Maison Paul Poiret in Rue Pasquier. The couturier causes a sensation by promoting light dresses with high waists which obviate the need to wear a corset.

1909   Paul Poiret moves his business to a handsome 18th-century residence, with courtyard and garden, in Avenue d'Antin (now Avenue Franklin-Roosevelt).

1911   Fashion parades are organized in all the European capitals to promote the name of Poiret. The couturier diversifies by launching Les Parfums de Rosine, a firm set up to create the first couturier perfumes. He also establishes a fabric printing workshop (employing among others Raoul Dufy) and L'Atelier Martine, a workshop devoted to the creation of decorative art: furniture, objects, textiles, and so on. Poiret's style generally veers in the direction of the Orient. He introduces the culotte skirt. On 24 June at Avenue d'Antin he throws an unforgettable party, one that would never be rivalled in the annals of Parisian social life: 'The Thousand and Second Night'.

1914   Private Poiret joins the army as a tailor and is attached to the 119th Infantry Regiment.

1918	He organizes the cutting and tailoring of military uniforms by civilian manufacturers.
1919	He is demobilized with the rank of captain. By now he is 39 and has three children. On 1 August, at his first postwar collection, he presents 250 models. He is at height of his talent as a dress designer, but already running into trouble.
1920	He opens a second branch in Cannes.
1922	Creates costumes for Broadway shows, most memorably the Ziegfield Follies.
1924	Maison Poiret leaves the Avenue d'Antin for the Rond-Point des Champs-Elysées.
1925	He decorates the three barges 'Délices', 'Amours', and 'Orgues' for the Exposition des Arts Décoratifs.
1926	The sale of his collections does not raise enough money to pay off his debts, and his fashion house has to be wound up.
1927	Publishes the publicity album *Pan* and acts in Colette's *La Vagabonde*.
1929	The salon at the Rond-Point des Champs-Elysées closes its doors.
1930-1934	Publishes *En Habillant l'Epoque*, *Revenez-y* and *Art et Phynance*.
1947	Paul Poiret dies in poverty and almost forgotten just after a retrospective exhibition of his paintings in Paris had shown his own work to the general public for the first time.

Bibliography

En Habillant l'Epoque by Paul Poiret, Editions Grasset, 1930. Better than a memoir, an entracing book about the creation of fashion, and the life and imagination of a man whose talent was multifaced.
Poiret le magnifique by Jack Palm White, Editions Payot, 1986. The author knew Madame Poiret well. With great respect and amdirable care he has spent more than ten years studying this exceptional person. An exemplary biography.
Poiret by Yvonne Deslandres, Thames and Hudson, 1987. A handsome, fully illustrated book, written by the creator of the Musée Galliera, Musée de la Mode de la Ville de Paris. Her knowledge of her subject is comprehensive.
Paul Poiret et Nicole Groult, maîtres de la mode Art déco (under Guillaume Garnier's direction), Musée de la Mode et du Costume, Palais Galliera, exhibition catalogue, July 5–October 12, 1986, Editions Paris Musées, 1986.

POIRET

Sleeveless evening dress in black gauze over white satin, with large motifs embroidered in black and white beads. The hem is edged with black velvet, 1910. © UFAC.

'Batik' and 'Negus', two evening coats by Poiret, 1911. Taken from *Art et décoration*, April 1911. Photo Steichen. © All rights reserved.

Illustration for a coat by Poiret, drawing by Georges Lepape, published in the *Gazette du bon ton*, no. 3, May 1920. © 1997 ADAGP.

'Son of heaven', 1923. Sleeveless dress in bright red velvet with waist-high side slits fastened by a black satin tie. Embroidered at the sides and round the neck with gold braid and a black satin bias. UFAC Collection. © UFAC.

'Les Robes de Paul Poiret', illustrations by Paul Iribe, 1908. © All rights reserved.

'Blida', 1911. Long satin sheath dress with a muslin overdress embroidered with a design of stylized bananas, lemons and pineapples in shades of green and gold. Taken from *Art et décoration*. Photo Steichen. © All rights reserved.

A forerunner of the prêt-à-porter of the great couture houses: evening dress in velvet and satin. This model was designed by Poiret for Liberty in 1933. Poiret, who by this time no longer had his own fashion house, signed a contract with both Liberty and Au Printemps to present several collections per year. © Victoria and Albert Museum.

Detail of opera cloak, ribbed silk, figured silk and metal threads, c. 1912. © Victoria and Albert Museum.

Fluid lines, high waist, bodice fastened with the stylized rose that was Poiret's trademark – some key elements in the Poiret revolution which took place during the years before the Great War. *Left:* House robe, drawing by Charles Martin c. 1911. Musée Galliera Collection, Musée de la Mode de la Ville de Paris. © All rights reserved.

Outfit with hobble skirt and bodice with basque, drawing by Erté, Summer, 1913. Musée Galliera Collection, Musée de la Mode de la Ville de Paris. © 1997 ADAGP.

Evening dress in bright red gauze embroidered with small gold bobbles over red crepe-de-chine, high-waisted empire line. © UFAC.

'Pompon', 1911. Sheath dress in blue velvet worn under a long tunic in cherry muslin sprigged with cretonne bouquets in green, white and red. Taken from *Art et décoration*, April 1911. Photo Steichen. © All rights reserved.

The illustrator Georges Lepape brought out a deluxe edition of his book *Les choses de Poiret vues par Lepape* (Poiret as seen by Lepape) in 1911. Perhaps a distant ancestor of the promotional catalogues created nowadays for designers by famous photographers. Sketch for an evening cloak by Lepape for the *Gazette du bon ton*. © 1997 ADAGP.

Dressing gown made in Bianchini-Férier's 'Fruit' brocatelle, a pattern designed by Dufy, 1923. © Musée Galliera Collection, Musée de la Mode de la Ville de Paris.

Madeleine Rodriguès, the actress, dressed by Poiret in *Le Fantôme du Moulin Rouge* (The Phantom of the Moulin Rouge) by René Clair, 1924. © Musée Galliera Collection, Musée de la Mode de la Ville de Paris.
Bedroom in the barge 'Amours' (the other two barges were named 'Délices' and 'Orgues'), designed for the Exposition Internationale des Arts Décoratifs in 1925. © Photo Lipnitzki-Viollet.

'It's Me', drawing by André Marty of an evening ensemble by Paul Poiret, 1922. © All rights reserved.
The great couturier choosing fabric from a range of ethnic material; he was the first designer in Paris to use traditional and ethnic fabrics so consistently. © All rights reserved.

'Batik'. Full-length evening cloak, falling from the shoulders and folded in at the sides. The collar and cuffs are trimmed with fur. Taken from Art et décoration, April 1911. Photo Steichen. © All rights reserved.
'Chez Poiret', two models illustrated by Georges Barbier, 1912. © Musée Galliera Collection, Musée de la Mode de la Ville de Paris.

Evening wear that plainly owes its inspiration to oriental dress; this outfit consists of a short muslin tunic worn over a skirt, 1912. © Victoria and Albert Museum.
A similar model drawn by Georges Lepape for the *Gazette du bon ton* in an illustration entitled 'The New Necklace', January 1913, Georges Lepape. © 1997 ADAGP.

A fantasy designed by Poiret, February 1920. © Archives de la Seine.
Oriental costume for the play The Minaret; skirt with two layers in embroidered muslin worn over a pair of harem pants, 1923. © Photo Roger-Viollet.

A gregarious and jovial man, Paul Poiret enjoyed organizing elaborate entertainments, often fancy-dress parties; he is seen here with some of his employees in the garden of his residence in Rue d'Antin, on the occasion of a St Catherine's Day ball. Photo Delphi. © UFAC.
A Persian party at the Poiret residence. *Fémina* titrage, 1912; drawing by Georges Lepape. © 1997 ADAGP.

'Racing at Longchamp', a dress with geometric pattern worn over a plain undergarment, 1923. Photo Seeberger.
Sketch for a coat from Poiret's workshop, c. 1912. © Musée Galliera Collection, Musée de la Mode de la Ville de Paris.

Jacques-Henri Lartigue, the painter and photographer, knew Poiret and brought his fiancée Bibi to his couture house. She is seen here wearing a coat designed for her by Poiret. Photo Jacques-Henri Lartigue, 1922. © Ministry of Culture, France.

'Fantasio', overcoat, 1921. Photo Gilbert René. © Archives de la Seine.
'Balloon', about 1920. High collar in blue velvet with leather buttons. © UFAC.

Black silk and wool coat trimmed with white leather and white fur, 1919.
Detail of the same coat. © Metropolitan Museum of Art.

Paul Poiret started the fashion for boots in all shapes and colours. Here his wife Denise wears a green duveteen jacket edged with braid of the kind worn by Moscow coachmen, a beige skirt, a white lawn blouse with a frill in Valenciennes lace, and a postilion hat in white wool. The dark green leather boots are by Cousin (in Rue de la Boétie). Photo taken at the New York Plaza Athena in 1913. © All rights reserved.
Black velvet dress with white lace collar and cuffs, inspired by Louis XIII, c. 1923. © Photo Roger-Viollet.

Detail of an afternoon dress in cherry velvet. Slashed sleeves and breast pocket. Buttonholes in gold thread and pink silk. © UFAC.
Detail of an evening coat in orange brocaded silk with oriental-style motifs, lined with shot silk. Fastened with large frogging in the same green as the lining and with six gold buttons, c. 1913. © UFAC.

Paul Poiret set up shop in 1925 at the Rond-Point des Champs-Elysées. He commissioned this wrought-iron grille from Edgar Brandt, the artist in metal. The doors, with their Art Deco ribbon feature around the frame, are still in place. © Lipnitzki-Viollet.
A coat in two colours, similar to the 'Balloon' coat, c. 1925. © Photo Lipnitzki-Viollet.

The many talents of Raoul Dufy, the painter and illustrator, fascinated Paul Poiret, in particular his colour sense and his draughtmanship. They worked together on a number of projects. Here the painter interpreted the couturier's gowns for the *Gazette du bon ton*, no. 4, May 1920. © 1997 ADAGP.

Tapestry shoe made at the Aubusson factory to a 17th-century design. Created for Paul Poiret by the great shoemaker André Perugia in 1924. © Photo Roger-Viollet.

'Manchu', a coat embroidered with large stylized floral motifs; the collar, wide sleeves and hem are trimmed with fur, 1921. Photo Gilbert René. © Musée Galliera Collection, Musée de la Mode de la Ville de Paris.
Evening coat in black silk with Japanese-style designs, c. 1925. Photo Richard Haughton. © Kyoto Costume Institute.

Coat created by Paul Poiret in 1927. His fashion house was by now closed and he had a part in a play, *La Vagabonde* by Colette. His co-stars were Colette and Marguerite Moreno. © Lipnitzki-Viollet.
Peggy Guggenheim, the American milionairess, was a keen patron of the avant-garde in the early 20th century. Here, in a photograph by Man Ray, she is wearing an oriental dress in gold lamé embroidered with multicoloured beads, designed by Paul Poiret. Her turban is Vera Stravinski. © 1997 ADAGP.

Renée, the model, in an evening dress with a long tunic and train, 1925. Photo Scaioni. © Courtesy The Condé Nast Publications Inc.
Paul Poiret had a passion for fragrances, and was the first couturier to launch his own range of perfume. Seen here, 'Harlequinade' is a mixture of cubism and the Orient. © Musée International de la Parfumerie, Grasse.

This evening dress, 'Longhi', with its three-cornered hat bound in gold, was inspired by the fetes and carnivals of Venice. © Photo Roger-Viollet.
'Am I Going to Be Early ?', drawing by Georges Lepape for the *Gazette du bon ton*, 1912. © 1997 ADAGP.

'Linzener', an evening dress designed for his wife by Paul Poiret, worn for the opening of Oasis in July 1919. The dress is made of silver fabric, and worn with mother-of-pearl earrings set with silver wire. Photo Delphi. © UFAC.
'Faun', 1919-1920. The bodice, held up by a cord round the neck, is in gold lamé with a plunging V-neck at the back. The skirt is fringed with monkey fur and gold beads. The shoes are also gold and the bird is by Brancusi. Photo Delphi. © UFAC.

Evening dress, black tulle sheath embroidered all over with brilliants, long white beads and strass. The dress is open down the sides and has a square train, 1907. © UFAC.
Renée, the model, in a sequined evening dress at Paul Poiret's Nouvel Hôtel in 1925. Photo Scaioni for *Vogue*, 1925. © Courtesy The Condé Nast Publications Inc.

The publishers would like
to thank for their help and
their invaluable contributions
to this book:

Joëlle Chariau (Galerie Bartsch &
Chariau), Françoise Vitu (Musée
Galliera), Madame Derra (Musée
International de la Parfumerie),
Rie Nii (Kyoto Costume Institute),
Martine Dastié (Association des
Amis de Jacques-Henri Lartigue),
Nicole Chamson (ADAGP),
Madame Lajournade (Roger-
Viollet), Marie-Hélène Poix
(UFAC) and Pierre-Yves
Butzbach (Telimage).